UNMASKYTP WORKBOOK

UnmaskYTP Workbook

Lessons Learned

DR. JAMES ARTHUR WILLIAMS

UnmaskYTP Publishing

UNMASKYTP PUBLISHING

For information, please visit our website
www.unmaskytp.us2.authorhomepage.com or *www.unmaskytp.com*

Unmask YTP Workbook
by Dr. James Arthur Williams

ISBN: 978-1-7351063-3-5

PUBLISHERS NOTE

CONTENTS

Introduction: 18 Exciting Lessons Learned

Lesson 1: The power in understanding your origin

Lesson 2: Blame no one for your choices

Lesson 3: Change your rhetoric and speak with veracity

Lesson 4: Develop an expectancy mindset

Lesson 5: Visualize what you want and walk in it

Lesson 6: Work, work, and work some more

Lesson 7: Fall forward with belief and stop looking back

Lesson 8: Be unapologetic about your purpose

Lesson 9: Self-educate daily and never stop learning

Lesson 10: Train your body like an athlete

Lesson 11: Find your hidden spirituality

Lesson 12: Just be in the moment

Lesson 13: Seek blessings, lessons, and opportunities

Lesson 14: Stop playing God and be the change

Lesson 15: Live life with vigor and concentrated focus

Lesson 16: Embrace and meet your fears head on

Lesson 17: Give earnestly and presume to receive nothing

Lesson 18: Release ourselves to the fact that we know nothing

Poems

Thanks to God, my wife, kids, parents, brothers, family, and friends for inspiring me to be limitless and to giving my life to inspire others to be limitless! I will continue to live hard, unconditionally love, and be at peace with all of you sentient beings. This book is dedicated to all of you limitless souls, so I implore you all to be better than your best and to be limitless.

| 1 |

Lessons Learned

UNMASKYTP WORKBOOK

Dr. James Arthur Williams

2

The Great Unmasking

Lessons will be employed to promote practical skills for individuals at all phases of development, enabling you to turn these lessons into applicable transferrable skills that will enhance your life, both personally and professionally. I will coach you along the way with **life points**, thought-provoking questions, suggestion tactics, and real-life examples and success stories to guide you along the mysterious odyssey.

We never stop dreaming and evolving, as we are invariably seeking a greater awareness of self. With this notion of perpetual evolution, we must never disregard this unmasking concept as irrelevant. Normally, the masked individuals are those who repudiate the truth and dismiss the need to unmask. Unmasking will lead us on the right paths of our journeys. Our journeys will be thrilling as we begin to unmask and live a unique life predestined for us…so come on, let's get started because an even better life awaits all of us.

Lesson 1: The power in understanding your origin

Where are we from? What are we made for? What is our purpose? These questions have plagued many of us throughout different phases of our lives, such as when we graduated from high school or college, exited the military, switched jobs or changed careers, lost a love one, ended a relationship, or felt like life was not worth living. As babies, we are guided by a higher spirit and entrusted to parents who hopefully raise us to be productive citizens and beings who exhibit love to everyone. The conundrum is that our environment (i.e., school, friends, parents, teams, and religions) shapes the manner in which we tend to think, but we adopt those thoughts as our own and inadvertently mask ourselves to our godliness and to our hidden potential.

We must remember our origins begin from an infinite source that cannot be fully explained by any finite man. We can guide and ignite passions that lead one to the source, but that esoteric knowledge and understanding have to be sought individually. This prompts us to dig deeper to find our origin and reason for being, causing us to examine self with the Socratic Method. We have to ask questions that urge for a deeper analysis of our metacognition or awareness of ourselves, so we can find the answers that escort us to our authentic selves and godly nature. All of us have God in us, even if we choose not to believe in a religion; we must acknowledge that something much greater than self created us with an infinite source of power and limitless energy.

Please answer these questions and reflect on your answers:

1. Who are you and how do you know this is the real you?

    ____

2. What are your values and why are they your values?

    ____

    ____

3. How do your values line up with what you currently do?

    ____

4. What is the "why" behind your actions?

____
____
____
____
____
____
____

Life Point

I discovered my origin when I rejected the idea of manmade religion.
I am not suggesting you all follow my decision; our treks are individualized and enigmatic experiences. When I declined to participate in
dogma practices derived from man's interpretations and logic, this led

me to research all religions, the origins of religions and to examine Jesus's life. This led me to focus on exhibiting Jesus' characteristics, even if it meant opposing religion and acting contrary to my previous understanding of God. This journey was mine, and it was very hard, but the outcome was rewarding, empowering, and liberating. It enabled me to unmask to a relationship and to develop a real heart for God, creating a true God-consciousness to unmask my true origin.

Lesson 2: Blame no one for your choices

Every decision comes from our thinking, which leads to our heart. When the thought is embedded in our heart, it will ultimately lead to an action, either positive or negative. We are all given volition in this life and no matter the circumstance; we are forced to take the easy route or to travel the harder path. The easy route propels us to blame others for all of our mistakes, issues, and problems as they occur in this existence, while the hard trek causes us to embrace our problems and to find some culpability in them, even if it is as simple as our response to a conundrum.

We must take accountability for fractured relationships, for so-called failures, for poor decisions, and for anything that does not work out in our favor. We should seek inwardly prior to examining outwardly. For example, if we open the door for someone and they fail to say thank you, we cannot assume it is fair to curse or say something inappropriate to combat their level of impoliteness. It is our choice to become upset or annoyed; we cannot blame them for our behavior. Every action sparks a reaction, so we must think proactively before we react impulsively.

Please answer these questions and reflect on your answers:

1. Who do you blame for your past shortcomings, mistakes, or other issues? Why?

   ____

2. Think deeply – what could you have done to rectify a past blame?

   ____

   ____

3. Be honest – what was your culpability in some past mistakes?

   ____

   ____

4. How has this awareness of accountability made you more prepared for the future issues?

____

____

____

____

____

____

Life Point

I contrived an acronym to guide my thought process prior to acting or making a decision. The acronym is coined **PMTA: pray, meditate, think,** and **act**. **Praying** requires conscious awareness, and I employ this principle to focus on goodness that wishes love and kindness upon all humans and situations. I start prayers with well wishes for others and conclude with well wishes for self and how my progress can be used to infuse others. **Meditation** brings me to an absent thought of nothingness to clear my mind, using it as a reset button.

I count to 10 while taking 10 synonymous deep breaths, and I repeat over and over until my mind feel well rested. **Thinking** is something that should be applied often throughout the day, keeping a small notepad to record your ideas and to subscribe to positive aphorisms. This process enables you to be mentally rested and to **act** accordingly in any given circumstance. We must watch our actions verbally and non-verbally, providing uncomplaining ethos and positive energy throughout every environment. Try to take the time to understand your flaws and shortcomings and employ **PMTA** to unmask from blame.

Lesson 3: Change your rhetoric and speak with veracity

Our words, syntax, and passion of delivery determine how impactful and inspirational our messages can be to our audience. Our spectators can be one person or millions of people. I believe in an infinite source that suggests the world was spoken into existence. "For God spoke, and it was done" (Psalm 33:9). Some rely on energy and science to explain evolution, and all communities agree on something greater than self; and both refer to the power of thought and speech.

The conundrum is that many people converse before conceptualizing the impact of their words and prior to selecting words with fastidious care. When we take the time to analyze a situation, we can proactively organize our words that will enlighten others and promote love. We must talk in a loving way that is specific to the person or persons we come in contact with, employing honest and intense rhetoric (e.g., in a way that shows you are invested in the current conversation) in the process.

Please answer these questions and reflect on your answers:

1. How do you speak to people? Does it promote positive or negative responses? Please explain your responses.

   ____

2. How do you select your words and why do you use that particular arrangement?

   ____

   ____

3. Explain how you spoke something into existence. How did you speak with passion and belief?

   ____

4. What will you do to speak love into confrontational and negative situations in the future?

____

____

____

____

____

____

____

Life Point

Immediately, we should seek our fault or error when situations go awry. We all have faced quandaries, and at times, they have energized us to act out of character; some people refer to it as blacking out or seeing red. Whatever the reason, they are all just excuses and reasons to conduct self inappropriately. I cursed at someone for calling me an unsuitable name, telling people he disrespected me and should not have spoken to me like that. It was all about me—disrespect and the way he spoke. This impacted my ego or self-worth, so I felt insignificant in his eyes, no longer viewing him as a person who deserves love.

This individual could have just found out some devastating news, such as a diagnosis of a terminal illness or the passing of a loved one. I became aware of the fact that I was wrong for reacting in a negative fashion. I should have not expected this individual to treat me a certain way, but instead, focused on treating him with love and compassion rather than convictions. Be the love to unmask love in every situation.

Lesson 4: Develop an expectancy mindset for your personal success

We have to believe in ourselves if we expect other people to be inspired to follow us or to believe in us. We must know where we are going prior to establishing an expectancy mindset, understanding our aim or intended goal. Our end goal must not be defined by other people's opinions; we must define and articulate our personal success to self. Our lives are individualized and set to make an impact for a finite time, so other people's ideas for our lives will never fully satisfy us if it is not our unmasked potential. Most people focus the majority of their time and energy on trying to determine what is needed for someone to become successful while they are still masked to their true potential.

Masking themselves with their wealth, houses, cars, spouses, children, clothes, etc. may create temporary happiness, but this never enables them to fill themselves with true joy. Joy that lasts when loved ones pass on, relationships or careers end, health wanes, or finances dwindle. Yet, when our personal success is tied to our internal growth, mentally, physically, and spiritually, we will learn to expect personal success in everything we do and in every situation that arises.

Please answer these questions and reflect on your answers:

1. Write and describe your honest thoughts about yourself. Do you believe you are a gifted-thinker, beautiful person, likeable individual, or potential game-changer in this life? Please explain your responses.

   ____

2. What is your definition of success? How does that definition align with your personal definition of success? Please explain your response.

   ____

   ____

3. What masked successes have you hidden behind? Why?

____

4. What is the difference between joy and happiness? What are
    you doing to find or to continue to live life with unlimited
    joy?

____
____
____
____
____
____
____

Life Point

Success is an ambiguous concept for many people. Many of us define
success by our titles (i.e., professor, engineer, doctor, lawyer, etc.), ma-

terialistic things, or religions; but your success is greater than all of those manmade concepts. Titles and materialistic items do not give or take value away from us and religions do not create our personal relationship with God. All of them bring us to a point of happiness, but a seeking of something even greater arouses us to unlimited joy.

I focus on pleasing God (or, for some of us, a source much greater) that pulls me to all truth—the truth within and the truth in this physical realm, making me understand the power of missing someone when they die but celebrating their transition over to something greater and better than here. My success comes in knowing I will die one day, so I am free to love and to give my best until that day comes—being my personal success. When we know for certain we will die, we will be able to unmask to our personal success.

Lesson 5: Visualize what you want and walk in it

Most athletes, actors, innovators, and astute business leaders report visualizing an action in their minds long before it ever manifests in the physical realm. In an interview, Michael Jordan stated that he performed moves over and over in his mind and envisioned his success on the basketball court before taking one shot in the game. MJ would torch and torment defenders night-after-night, executing moves that he practiced and visualized in his mind, to give him a competitive edge. When we visualize something, we develop the wherewithal to confidently construct an apparatus that brings our ideas to fruition.

Our ability to visualize an idea or creation provides clarity in our awareness, and it fortifies our self-assurance as we work towards fulfilling our conceptualized dreams. Walking in it causes us to move with affirmation and faith, but it cannot occur if we do not know what the end goal is. Without a visualized outcome, we tend to walk aimlessly, stripping us of a specific purpose.

Please answer these questions and reflect on your answers:

1. What was your childhood dream and did you fulfill it? Why or why not?

2. What are your current dreams? How are you working towards acquiring them?

3. What is the most important personal dream (e.g. only about you…no family can be included in a personal dream) you have a desire to achieve before you expire? What would you give up for it?

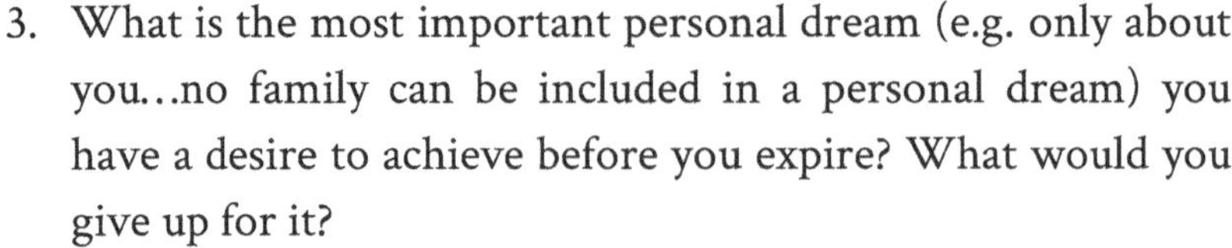

4. Name one dream that you will work towards today. Explain
    how you will commit to it.

____

____

____

____

____

____

Life Point

We are trained to capture other people's dreams as our own, causing
us to lose our identity and to mask our hidden desires. We are also
brainwashed to place other people above ourselves. Many of us focus
on making other people happy and on making their dreams come true
while sacrificing our own happiness. From this day forward, you must

come first if you have a desire to give your best friendship, love, and compassion to others. On airplanes, they inform passengers to don their mask before attempting to help their children, family members, or others put on their masks.

If the plane loses oxygen and we try to put the mask on our child prior to self, we might lose consciousness and, ultimately, our child will suffer dearly for our consequences. When we love others more than ourselves, ultimately others will suffer as well because they are not getting the best of us; they are getting someone void of our individualized oxygen. We have to breathe life into our dreams prior to walking in our contrived purpose. Visualization is a must if we have a desire to unmask and to walk to a particular purpose.

Lesson 6: Work, work, and work some more

Hard work is the building block of the Roman empire, America, and any other powerful nation. Work must remain continuous, causing us to never become complacent. Complacency builds mediocrity and creates a habit loop of laziness. The greatest difference between hard work and complacency is that hard work allows us to sleep well, but complacency enables us to have restless sleep and too much idle time (Proverbs 19:15). We must be incessant workers, transforming into human ants. Ants are diligent and resilient in their work efforts, remaining locked in to their set objectives. Many of us have become accustomed to receiving compliments and praise to give our work contentment. People who are committed to work rarely take the time to relish in others' praise about their work; they are busy trying to augment their work daily, never resting in any gratification—loving the process instead—the work.

Please answer these questions and reflect on your answers:

1. Explore your view of hard work. Is it rewarding or taxing? Explain your response.

   ____

2. How have you settled for complacency in your life? How did it make you feel?

   ____

   ____

3. What tactics have you employed or will you employ to remove complacency from your life? Why have you chosen these tactics?

   ____

4. What do you hate to do? Please explain the process and discuss some things you could do to try to fall in love with the process.

____

____

____

____

____

____

Life Point

We must always find ways to improve ourselves, personally and professionally, meaning we never stop working on evolution. I wake up
early in the morning to meditate, to pray, to study scripture, to read
intellectual text, and to train my body before engaging in professional
work. One must work our minds, bodies, and spirits daily, yielding to
something much greater than this world. Working out must be a committed and conscious thought if we intend to unmask a love for hard
work.

Lesson 7: Fall forward with belief and stop looking back

We must have crazy belief to unmask from our old selves or from our old paradigms. Crazy belief requires us to stand tall in many situations, to walk alone and to not fear being rejected by the masses who follow trends that might lead them to a path of normalcy. The notion to fall forward means we trust in a higher force and in self to fall into our hidden potential. When we use all of our energies to fall forward, we do not possess the momentum to look back for support. We become an unstoppable train, moving with force and relying on conductors to stop it, God and us.

Power is constantly coursing through our dispositions, but many of us never tap into that latent power because we place our trust in mere man. Falling forward can propel us into a hidden spiritual realm that provides us with the grace promised to us by Jesus. Truly I say to you, you who believe in me will be able to do the same things as I (Jesus), even greater because I am going back to the father who sent me, living you a spirit that leads to all truth. There is a powerful spirit in all of us that will inspire us to fall forward and to stop seeking the comforting support of others.

Please answer these questions and reflect on your answers:

1. Explain a time when you had to believe for something and it came to fruition. How did you feel?
   ____

2. What does crazy belief mean to and do you have it in some areas of your life? Please explain your response.
   ____
   ____

3. In what ways do you feel powerful and in what ways do you feel insignificant?

____

4. Describe how you plan to feel powerful in all that you do.

____
____
____
____
____
____
____

____

Life Point

This lesson is not advising you to tackle life alone. We all need support to grow and to learn. I am urging you to stop looking back when the infinite source has given you the authority and wherewithal to press forward with no assistance from others. When it is time to sprint, we must gather ourselves and take off and never look back until we cross the finish line. I remember as a child going to the basketball court, hoping someone would ask me to play—but no one ever did.

I taught myself to dribble and to shoot, and eventually, I gained the confidence to play basketball with the big boys. I stopped looking for someone to ask, and I started getting up and walking to the court to play. I was willing to fall forward to unmask my hidden basketball potential.

Lesson 8: Be unapologetic about your purpose

As we grow and go further in life, people will reach up to bring us down or attempt to pull us back. People have odd ways of trying to make us feel bad about our purpose, suggesting that we have changed and/or are acting differently; this is a feeble aim to guilt us into staying still and to eschew walking in our purpose. As we pursue our purpose, we are ultimately walking in our personalized success. We should strive towards our purpose even when loved ones and friends object. We also must be quick to trim fat when negativity clouds or permeates our lives.

Most fat hangs onto us with no peculiar motive, impeding our progression as we work towards our set purpose. Removing fat ought to be swift, so we can maintain a sense of positivity as we traverse difficult terrain to achieve our objective. We must understand that some people are in our lives for a distinct reason and a distinctive season or seasons. Do not be afraid if it is time to move on from old relationships that include friends or family—be unapologetic and stop holding on to damaged luggage.

Please answer these questions and reflect on your answers:

1. Can you describe a time when people made you feel bad about your purpose? Why did you feel compelled to listen?

   ____

2. How did it feel when you lost some friends? Did you blame yourself? Please explain your responses.

   ____

   ____

3. What fat do you need to cut out of your life? Why does it need to be removed?

   ____

4. Describe how you plan on sticking to your purpose, even if
   people you love dearly are opposed to this purpose.

____

____

____

____

____

____

Life Point

Our purpose propels us to move with vigor, precluding us from identi-
fying the naysayers. However, when we do recognize a naysayer, those
detractors have a way of knocking us off our game and causing us to
invest time into their hate. We must fight this urge to invest our valu-
able time into trying to make them understand our journey; it is futile

and a true waste of time. As I wrote my book, I tried to write it in a manner that did not offend certain individuals, but some of those individuals were still offended instead of realizing it is my book and my perspective. I wrote several versions before speaking the absolute truth and disregarding how it might displease others.

I had to acknowledge that my purpose to galvanize people to unmask to their true potential was more pertinent than the emotions of antagonists, energizing me to trim the fat and to remove the negativity. Cut away the fat, so you can see and unmask to your true potential.

Lesson 9: Self-educate daily and never stop learning

Learning is a lifelong process; it never ends. We will be edifying ourselves until we expire. It is imperative that we embrace this notion because our brains are muscles. When muscles are not worked, muscles atrophy and become a hindrance more than a blessing to us. Another consequential idea to remember is that we should rely on self-education more than education received from outside sources.

Individuals who develop a level of mastery in any skill improve their dexterity when they practice and study alone. This is a prime example of one's ability to self-educate. Self-education drives us to seek additional information about our skill sets. This endeavor should become a daily feat to create a Habit Loop, as discussed by Charles Duhigg. For example, the still of the morning serves as our **cue**, reading and studying works as our **routine**, and conceptualizing a new theory functions as our **reward**.

Please answer these questions and reflect on your answers:

1. Describe your way of staying intellectually fresh. What are your mediums for learning new theories and data?

    ____

2. How have you embraced lifelong learning into your daily routine? Can you explain the rewards being extracted from this pursuit?

    ____

    ____

3. What areas of your life do you feel atrophy has set in? Math? Reading? Writing? Please explain your response in detail.

    ____

4. Elaborate on how you plan to self-educate on a daily basis. What will you add to your routine? How will you make time for learning and training your mind?

Life Point

Wake up vitalized and excited about the opportunity to take part in another day. Then, utilize that spark to open a book, even if you read one sentence, one paragraph, or one page; you know more than you did know prior to perusing that text. I invest an hour of reading before I watch television or pop open my laptop, using my vitality for life as my **cue**, reading as a teacher (e.g., cogitating over material and digging deeper to understanding a deeper meaning) as my **routine**, and sharing the novel information with my family and friends as my **reward**. This information sharing unmasked me to self-educate, so I can aspire to greatness.

Lesson 10: Train your body like an athlete

We know a mind is a terrible thing to waste, but a wasteful body can carry a well-developed brain only for so long. Training is a must, and researchers suggest that working out enhances brain memory and critical thinking skills. However, I propose we train like an athlete because athletes do not work out to maintain health or to do mundane activities; they train to be extraordinary and to be the best in their given sport. They accept the notion of being better than their best.

As we continue to unmask, we understand that it is nothing mundane or average about our lives. We are extraordinary and amazing, so there should be nothing that stops us from training and improving our exterior. To train like an athlete, we build a proactive body that can handle contingencies and distinctions in game maneuvers. Training our bodies gives us an opportunity to acquire new information and compounding data while ruminating on a much deeper level.

Please answer these questions and reflect on your answers:

1. How often do you train your body? Explain ways you find enjoyment from some of your workouts.

    ____

2. Do you work out to look great or do you work out for a lifestyle? What is the difference between workout and lifestyle?

    ____

    ____

3. I challenge you to work out for a couple of days and test yourself on some newly acquired knowledge. How did your learning development improve from this practice?

    ____

4. What steps will you take to improve your health daily? Explain your tactics to training like an athlete.

____

____

____

____

____

____

____

Life Point

Healthy living is essential to brain growth and to creating a productive lifestyle. We should find workouts and training that fit our lifestyles. I was taking blood pressure medication and eating recklessly until I decided to train like an athlete. We must understand that to train like an athlete, we must also eat like an athlete—healthy eating is a crucial key. I put myself on a rigorous diet and a strict training regimen until I dropped 43 pounds and was removed from blood pressure medication.

I trained like an athlete and unmasked to a hidden healthy body of abs and detailed muscle definition.

Lesson 11: Find your hidden spirituality

Mind, body, and spirit are elements needed to unmask to our true potential. We all have levels of spirituality in us. Spirituality is the understanding that a force much greater than self exists and permeates its spirit in all situations and life forms. It is an understanding that as long as energy exists, this infinite source will invariably remain in control. When we view ourselves as insignificant to this life, our spirituality remains dormant and ineffective in the physical.

It is our job to awaken that enlightened spirit. Spirituality is more substantial than religion and the way any man trains you to think about God or this unlimited source of life. We should conceptualize the fact that some religions attempt to sell us on the idea that a man with limited knowledge can tell us how to serve a God with infinite understanding. It is tantamount to a toddler attempting to tell other toddlers how to understand intricate details about their parents.

We are babies who are trying to lead other babies to a heightened awareness of God, when we should be urging people to seek the source for themselves and to cease relying on seers and religious institutions to know God. Churches should be implored as support or resource centers rather than informing us to serve places. Seers and a religious institution killed Jesus, and Jesus never charged us to create a religion after him.

Please answer these questions and reflect on your answers:

1. What do you believe in? God? Infinite source? Science? Self? Nothing? Why?

   ____

2. Name a time in your life when you felt a higher spirit evoked. What happened in that particular situation?

   ____

   ____

3. What is your definition of religion, relationship, and spirituality? Which avenue or paths rule your life? Why?

____

4. Explain how you plan to be more spiritual in your daily life. How will you use this plan to impact you, personally and professionally?

____
____
____
____
____
____
____

Life Point

I found God when I lost my religion. Initially, I relied on church to inspire me to conduct myself in a godly fashion, but I found myself frustrated and vexed by the traditions, rules, and constant judgments. This forced me to seek an understanding of God for myself. Seek first God's kingdom and God's righteousness, and all these things will be given unto you (Matthew 6:33). I wake around 5:45 am and use the first five minutes to meditate and then I study the scriptures until I feel satisfied in my spirit.

I no longer set rules on my studying; I followed my spirit. This spirit led me to my truth and to an in-depth understanding of God that offered me all the desires of my heart. I was guided to play professional arena football, speak to small and large audiences, manage businesses, act on television shows, create my own business and concept, and serve as a professor at a major research institution. This is the first time in my life I feel liberated and as if God is walking with me and providing me with an abundance of favor.

I unmasked a godly love and spirituality that advised me to serve others with all my heart.

Lesson 12: Just be in the moment

The present matters more than any other time in history. We can study the past and learn from it, but we cannot travel back in time to alter it. We can prepare and strategically plan for the future, but we do not know how things will truly play out. Yet, when we concentrate all our exertion on the present moment, it permits us to produce our best self and free self for that particular time. The Theory of Relativity postulates that speed and time can be different for each person due to our frame of reference. I am enamored by this theory; I just see it a little differently.

Being in the moment is the Theory of Relativity to me, meaning the only thing that matters or is relevant is the time and space we occupy in our present moment. We cannot worry about situations and people when they are not in our current space because our concerns will not change what happens in those disparate spaces. However, as we focus on our present moment, we can only provide our best intellect, spirit, and body to that person we interact with or situation we maneuver in.

Please answer these questions and reflect on your answers:

1. Describe a time when you were being in the moment. How did you know and how did it feel?

   ____

2. What are some things in your past that you cannot let go? Why?

   ____

   ____

3. What are some issues in the future stressing you, such as death, retirement, money, etc.? Why?

   ____

4. Explain what you will do moving forward to conquer your fears and worries about past guilt and future issues. How will being in the moment assist you?

Life Point

I remain in the present and adopt my Theory of Relativity—nothing else matters in my present space and time - nothing. My approach is closely tied to the Law of Correspondence, which implies there is a truth in correspondence between laws and the phenomena of various planes of Being and Life. I interpret this to mean that the spiritual law suggests God is ubiquitous, and God's omnipresence connects to all spaces where life exists.

This information charges me to pray for a mental, physical, and spiritual commitment to engage in the present, producing an imbued love in all occurrences. It propels me to cut off the TV and to find a silent place when someone phones me, so I can supply that person with my best and undivided attention. I pray for God to furnish me with the energy and focus needed to stay engaged and to never be distracted from the moment. This attitude permits us to unmask our supreme being for the current moment. Remember, the only thing that matters is what you are doing in the NOW.

Lesson 13: Seek blessings, lessons, and opportunities in everything

Everything happens for a reason, but it is our job to seek the blessings, lessons, and opportunities for growth. There are life lessons in every circumstance; it does not matter if the affair is deemed good or bad. The greatest enemy, self, convinces us to believe so-called bad situations are the end of the world, gripping us with fear of worry and in many circumstances, guilt. We must develop short-term memories when it comes to so-called failures and successes. I refer to them as "so-called" because both are contrived from our perceptions or the perceptions of different people.

However, surface-level successes or failures are not indicative of true blessings, lessons, and opportunities for evolution. If someone achieves their pinnacle of success and starts to regress, they have missed an opportunity to appreciate their heightened position, failed to connect the importance of hard work and diligence, and overlooked the opportunity to be even better. We acquire blessings in simple conversations; such as the blessing in simply being able to speak. We learn lessons from losing, understanding what does not work and conceptualizing what might work. Any so-called failure is always a chance for expansion.

Please answer these questions and reflect on your answers:

1. Describe areas in your personal and professional life that offer distinct blessings, lessons, and opportunities for development.

    ____

2. What blessings are you grateful for in your life?

    ____

    ____

3. Name some difficult situations in your life that taught you lessons and enhanced opportunities.

____

4. What strategies will you employ to acknowledge your blessings, learn new lessons, and improve opportunities (personally and professionally)?

____
____
____
____
____
____
____

Life Point

I perform outside meditation to connect my mind and body with nature. Once I rouse from my meditative state, I scan my environment for life, in hope of finding a blessing. I was blessed with analyzing the diligence and work ethic of ants; they stay focused and never stop moving. I decided to place my hand in one of the ant's path, and the ant kept maneuvering to avoid this obstacle while maintaining focus and commitment to complete his task. I discovered blessings and lessons come from all life forms. Those ants taught me to respect all life, so I try to never kill anything, unmasking me to value small and big things in life—all things matter and all things offer blessings.

Lesson 14: Stop playing God and be the change

Remove all judgments and expectations of dissimilar people. When we attempt to judge, we inadvertently function as God, informing people about what is right or wrong for their particular lives. The only person we should try to ameliorate is self because change lies within us—not in our judgments of disparate humans. The infinite source has all control and unlimited power, so we must terminate all desire to want to command people and to govern situations. Instead, we must find commonalities with all humans and release a desire to dictate their life decisions. When we find commonalities, we stop seeing people as objects and begin to visualize them as real tangible sources of existence and energy. Without commonalities, we produce standards and expectations manufactured in our minds, causing us to become vexed when others fall short—anger, frustrations, and hostility are soon to follow. Yet, individuals who seek out commonalities can focus energy there instead of seek to find fault in one's differences. Some basic and safe commonalities to use are sports, movies, music, family, military, travel, and any fun or exciting activities or things.

Please answer these questions and reflect on your answers:

1. Who have you judged in the past? What happened from that experience? Did you develop dislike or hatred for that person? Did it hurt or help your relationship?

   ____

2. Name a time when you had to relinquish control over a relationship or situation. What was the outcome? Positive or negative and why?

   ____

   ____

3. How have you utilized personal changes to stop judgments of people who look, think, or might act differently than you?

What joy did you get from this experience?

____

4. Explain how you will employ commonalities to start a con-
    versation with a random person whom you perceive as dif-
    ferent from you.

____
____
____
____
____
____
____

Life Point

I had to relinquish expectations of self and that encouraged me to stop
having expectations for other people. Once I removed those barriers,

I was not able to feel disappointed in self and to get upset with other people. I embraced people's great qualities and so-called flaws, and I stopped trying to change them, allowing them to be who they desired to be. For example, if you wave at someone, and they decide to refrain from waving back, your flesh might urge you to feel bothered or react in a negative fashion.

Yet, if you would have waved with no expectations of the certain person waving back, you would likely have been poised and impervious to their failure to wave back. This enables you to unmask all judgments and to exert energy to personalized change that leads you to be better than your best.

Lesson 15: Live life with vigor and concentrated focus

Life is filled with unused time. We rarely use all of our time with a concentrated focus. Many elements in our lifetime distract us from living our lives with vigor and truth. This brings up the notion that we can think ourselves happy if we can quell all of the anxiety from past experiences and future probabilities. Our past guilt can handcuff us to previous issues, which are unfixable, and this impedes us from being focused in the present. The present is a gift, and we can only unwrap that gift with passion when we are truly engaged and focused.

Many of us have opened tangible gifts on Christmas, birthdays, etc.; but we tended to open some gifts with minimal enthusiasm because our minds were distracted by another gift or expectation of something "better". This poor attitude shifts us out of focus and robs us of our zeal for life. It is crucial that we choose happiness and excitement as we venture through life, so we can capture the moment with concentrated focus. We must not surrender to our emotions and submit to anger, frustration, and bitterness, which pull us farther and farther away from a razor-sharp focus. Regardless of our beliefs, it is our choice to attack our existence with vigor and concentrated focus.

Please answer these questions and reflect on your answers:

1. Do you get excited about life? If so, in what ways? If not, what is stopping you?

   ____

2. What would you be willing to devote all of your time to? Why? What makes this endeavor special?

   ____

   ____

3. Name some things that require detailed focus in your life. How does your focus improve the overall outcome? Please

explain your response.

____

4. How will you start your day and future days with vigor and
    how will you stay in the moment with concentrated focus?

____
____
____
____
____
____
____

Life Point

I wake up and give thanks to God or our infinite source for allowing
me to have another day to inspire someone and to hopefully lead individuals to their untapped potential. Notice, I do not start with detailed

thoughts about myself; my awareness is on the service I can offer others because my maker created me for a higher purpose than satisfying myself. I am also grateful for all of my talents and abilities and my inner desire to live life with vigor. Once I give thanks, I force myself to wear an authentic smile.

Immediately, I begin praying for love, peace, and happiness of family members, friends, enemies, and future encounters. This enables me to walk into new environments with an expectancy of being a blessing to someone and to staying in the present with their physical and spiritual being. This preparation infuses me with an abundance of joy, which guides me to saturate environments with vigor that unmask me to concentrated and committed focus.

Lesson 16: Embrace and meet your fears head on

Our existence should consist of just being and flowing with the rhythm of life, evoking the law of rhythm, which postulates the truth that everything is in constant degree of motion. We can conclude from this declaration that there will be easy roads to travel and difficult barriers to overcome in our beings. Our predicament is how we react to the challenges and successes. Many times, we convert those abstract ideas into intangible and tangible fears. We might graduate from high school and construct fears about the difficulty of college and life in general.

We might not have the money to pay a bill, and we panic about our credit and preconceived embarrassment. Some people might develop a nasty cough and stress by convincing themselves it is something medically serious. Our alternative is to embrace fear with passion and a concentrated focus to rise above our impediments. Fear is an abstract opinion formulated in our psyches, so we must understand fear is not real; and we have the power to embrace and to meet our created fears with the self-assurance of obliterating it.

Please answer these questions and reflect on your answers:

1. What are your deepest fears? Why have decided to embrace them as fears?

   ____

2. How have your fears stopped you from taking risks or experiencing certain things in life?

   ____

   ____

3. Name some fears that you never recognized as issues, such as being afraid to try specific foods, petting a dog, running from snakes, scurrying from conversations, etc. What makes them so scary?

   ____

4. What fear will you meet today? What is your action plan and
    how will you attempt to attack your fears in the future?

____

____

____

____

____

____

____

Life Point

I embraced this fact, and it has changed my existence immensely: I will
die one day, and I might possibly die today. I wake every day with the
notion that this could be my last day, so I convince myself I will live it
to the fullest and be better today than I was yesterday. Once we conquer the fear of death, we start to live because when and how we die

becomes irrelevant—our existing in the moment becomes germane to our desire to quell fears.

I overcame the fear of heights, individuals' opinions, loss of a loved one, so-called failures, and snakes (even though I am still not a fan of the last one). God or our infinite source of life and energy did not give us a spirit of fear; instead, we were provided a disposition of truth and sovereign dominion over negative thoughts and humanistic worries (2 Timothy 1:7). Our role is to embrace fear and unmask to an acknowledgement that life flows in perfect rhythm with our current state of being – i.e., love our fears to their nonexistence.

Lesson 17: Give earnestly and presume to receive nothing back

We are here to serve others. Serving is not predicated on mere finances. Servitude tests someone's willingness to give up things that they hold dear and near to their hearts. Some of us have a hard time relinquishing our time, but we are quick to sacrifice money. God measures our hearts, so we must offer something that evokes an invested heart. We should also give and expect nothing in return. A bevy of individuals give, but they also presume to receive a blessing for their sacrifices. This belief can create an insatiable greed of invariably wanting something back in return for your pleasantries, time, and distinctive offerings.

Another issue is that some people do not care about acquired blessings or recompenses, but they do expect extol or an appreciation for their self-presumed kind act. Our expectancy wipes away the love and compassionate component of any earnest deed, so we must shut down all desires and expectations of receiving anything in return. We must produce a paradigm that becomes enamored to blessing souls in an earnest fashion. We are seeking to stir up souls that can assuage impulses and conjectures of our flesh. The underlying theme is that we must never focus on what we might receive; our sole purpose should be skewed towards what we might be able to provide with genuine fondness.

Please answer these questions and reflect on your answers:

1. What are you passionate about giving to? Does this require time, effort, money, etc.?

   ____

2. What are you reluctant to give up? Why?

   ____

   ____

3. What do you give earnestly to and have no desire to receive anything back? Why are you so giving in this area?

____

4. Describe what actions you will take to earnestly give and to presume nothing back.

____
____
____
____
____
____
____

Life Point

I am tasking everyone with one simple undertaking: we must pay it forward. We have to commit to blessing random people for arbitrary reasons. For example, I grappled with patience, so I allowed a person at the back of the line to acquire my position if I was closer. I would suggest paying for someone's food behind you in the fast food line, holding the door for casual beings, giving someone a compliment, providing homeless individuals with socks, soaps, and food, and/or teaching individuals beneficial information. You should perform these things without expecting anything back, not even a thank you or smile, to unmask to genuine compassion and service.

Lesson 18: Release ourselves to the fact that we know nothing

This is one of the hardest lessons to comprehend. Sometimes our egos or our individualized notion of self-importance encourage us to believe we are experts and knowers of all when engaged in a particular topic, especially when we converse with individuals who are insufficient in those knowledge domains. This misguided perspective can create friction between upper-level management and frontline workers. However, Albert Einstein surmised his intellect derived from his desire to be passionately curious, making him a seeker of understanding from all situations and life sources. There is an old adage that suggests you should not be the wisest man in every room.

This inadvertently means you must alter your perspective and see circumstances and people through a new lens, a lens that strives to learn from everybody and everything. We can discover the wrong ways and right ways of doing things from every person and incident. One of our major conundrums is assuming what other people mean from our biased viewpoint, producing incorrect judgments in many events. We are not mind readers or predictors of the future, so we cannot accurately interpret someone's mind or know our present actions will serve as a boon to the future. When we release ourselves to the fact that we know nothing, we become seekers of everything—this brings us to the truth and the source of all wisdom, an infinite source of understanding.

Please answer these questions and reflect on your answers:

1. Name some people you thought you knew. What happened in those situations? Did they change or were your expectations set inappropriately? What lessons did you learn?

   ____

2. Describe a clueless situation you faced. Were you more receptive to learning? Please explain this condition.

____

____

3. Can you share a time when your know-it all attitude got the
   best of you? What did you learn from this experience?

   ____

4. In what ways will you seek new knowledge in all types of
   conversations and circumstances? How will you remove the
   mask of assuming you know things?

____

____

____

____

____

____

____

____

____

Life Point

In *Change Your Thoughts-Change Your Life: Living the Wisdom of the Tao*, Dr. Dyer explains God as the nothingness or no-thing-ness, explaining that we cannot confine God to a specific religion. I was drawn to his profound outlook and definitive take on God because I do not believe we can ever comprehend this unlimited source of life, energy, love, and power. When we buy into the opinion of us knowing nothing, we are secretly closer to this nothingness origin. I developed an inner desire to improve in my profession as a professor, so I sought to change my teaching approach.

I had to come to the end of self and admit I do not know the best ways to instruct my students, prompting me to enter teaching settings with an open perspective. I had students turn in anonymous surveys about my teaching—what they like, dislike, and would like to see more of. I performed this function for several classes, and they taught me to embrace a didactic approach, to teach concepts and life lessons. I also challenge my pupils to discuss and participate in classroom discussions, to edify me and to unmask me to exhibit an existence controlled by no-

thing-ness. This unmask us to our hidden godliness and our true potential.

Poems

TODAY I SHED A TEAR

Today I shed a tear while standing strong, proud, and bold as a black man with no fear;

Even though I look around and found not too many other black males standing near

None to follow me here and none to cheer;

Another brother pass on from gun violence, heads down, a few words spoken before they tap out some beer

So today I shed a tear, the picture is not so clear;

Some are unjustly judged, ridiculed, and left in the rear, so yes, I shed a tear;

Prison systems are packed and stacked, but many in society still live in fear;

I shed a tear because many inmates are victimized inside their concrete cell and demonized by society and prone to fail;

This life is hell for many, not knowing that blessings come in the form of plenty;

And most blessings, do not cost a penny, it cost a thought and purpose to serve something that represents an infinity;

So I shed a tear, not just for black brothers, but for all my other ethnic brothers and mothers struggling with self out of internal and external fear;

So today I shed a tear.

WE SEARCH

We search for peace, we search for opportunity; we search for love, we search for unity;

We search for many things to hide the depths of our internal pains, protruding our veins, driving us insane;

Searching like a lost puppy because we search in vain, we search without evolving;

We search without ever calling a name so great because subcon-
sciously we are content with earth being are heavenly state;
Blindly ignoring the fact that we all have a death date, thinking
life is about finding that one true soul mate;
We search and we search, keeping God confined to the brick-
and-mortar building of a church;
We search and we search for the same fate of returning to the
dirt; ashes to ashes and dust to dust;
We search and we search, forgetting that God is a must.

**Express yourself here with a poem about you and send it to me,
so I can add it to my website.**

Send your poem to truesuccess32@gmail.com and I will upload it to this website: www.unmaskytp.com

Currently, Dr. Williams serves as an associate professor (tenured) at the University of Tennessee and is the owner of UNMASKYTP, LLC, training domestic and international leaders to dwell in joy while seeking curiosity in every endeavor. He teaches mindfulness, various leadership tactics, and one-on-one coaching to build brighter leaders for the future. He has worked with leaders in Spain, South Korea, Bulgaria, China, and at many Fortune 100 companies.

Dr. Williams is also a professional actor, performing as Uncle Tom in *Into the Wilderness (SAG/movie)* and starring as Waco Collins in *Murder Chose Me.* He wrote two books, *From Thug to Scholar: An Odyssey to Unmask my True Potential* and *How to Get Abs like a Bodybuilder but Eat like a Fat boy.* He has also published over 15 scholarly articles and delivered over 30 presentations on emotional intelligence, soft skills, sports, leadership, employee training, mentorship, hospitality pedagogy, human resource management, and personal and professional development.

Dr. Williams grew up masked, selling drugs at 13 years of age, fathering two kids, dropping out high school, and living on the streets by 17 years old.

Dr. Williams earned six degrees (two doctorates), Ph.D. from Iowa State University. He honorably served the United States Air Force, winning Airman of the Year. He played professional arena football for the Raleigh Rebels (2005-2006). Dr. Williams has industry experience in the dental, banking, sales, pharmaceuticals, manufacturing, hotels, and education. He is also a *Certified Hospitality Educator and trainer.*

Dr. Williams has also spoke to over 100 unique audiences, and won numerous speech competitions for *Toastmaster's International*; served as a keynote speaker for Coffeewood Correctional Institution, public schools, colleges, fortune 500 companies, professional organizations. Dr. Williams was also recognized as a *Top 15 Emerging Scholar of 2019* by Diverse: Issues in Higher Education. Dr. Williams also was a featured speaker for TEDx UTK in 2019. Best international mentor for Chinese Hospitality Education Initiative for the 2019 national championship in Shanghai, China.

www.ingramcontent.com/pod-product-compliance
Lightning Source LLC
Chambersburg PA
CBHW050015040726
47599CB00014B/1398